365
Things
Every
Man
Should
Know

HARVEST HOUSE PUBLISHERS
Eugene, Oregon 97402

Published in association with the
literary agency of
Alive Communications,
P.O. Box 49068,
Colorado Springs, CO 80949.

365 THINGS EVERY MAN SHOULD KNOW

Copyright © 1993 by Doug Fields
Published by Harvest House Publishers
Eugene, Oregon 97402

Library of Congress Cataloging-in-Publication Data

Fields, Doug
    365 things every couple should know / Doug Fields.
        p.   cm.
    ISBN 1-56507-096-8
    1. Men—Humor.   2. American wit and humor.   I. Title.
    II. Title: Three hundred sixty-five things every man should know.
PN6231.M45F54   1993
818′.5402—dc20   93-18
                                                              CIP

Printed in the United States of America.

To my dad, James Fields:
The one most important gift you ever gave me
was your belief. I love you!

And to my son, Cody James:
I hope you grow up to love me as much
as I love my dad.

A special thanks to Carl Dreizler for your
invaluable input and ideas.

Introduction

This little book is filled with thoughts, ideas, and comments about things I wish I knew while I was growing up. Obviously these are not sure-fire recipes for success, and I'm not suggesting that if you follow all the advice in this book you'll be cool. But now that we're into the '90s, let's revisit some "traditionalisms" we might have missed or not yet heard!

Savor and enjoy *365 Things Every Man Should Know* . . . some should be laughed at, some should make you pensive . . . and tear out the pages that might just tick you off!

1

that he can strive to have
the wit of Bill Cosby,
the wisdom of Solomon,
and the understanding
of Ward Cleaver.

2

how to cook three good
meals on a Coleman stove.

❦

3

how to sew on a shirt
button.

❦

4

that success has more to do
with self-worth than with
net worth.

5

how to tuck his kids in bed
at night.

6

that small risks can bring great gains.

❧

7

Arnold Schwartzenegger did not build his physique from lifting beer cans.

❧

8

at least three good jokes.

9

how to be a positive
influence to a child who
has no father.

10

that he should
go get the hammer
when pounding a nail
rather than reaching for
the nearest hard object.

11

to call home
at least once a day
when on a business trip.

12

how to change a diaper—
even a messy one.

13

how to lose gracefully.

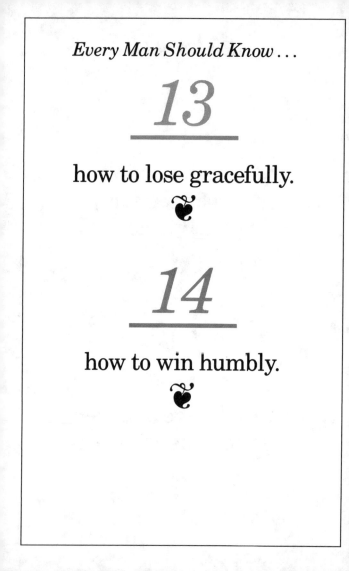

14

how to win humbly.

ways to hide
his bald spot with hair
from another part of
his head.

16

how to balance the
checkbook.

❧

17

how to work a video
camera.

❧

18

---

how to hug more people
than he does now.

19

---

the significance of the
crucifixion in his life.

20

that no matter
how old he gets, he is still
a child of God.

❧

21

the value of uncontrollable
laughter.

❧

22

the date
of his anniversary.

❧

23

the phone number of
the florist.

❧

24

how to be a good friend to
other men.

❧

25

that it won't hurt to help
her look for her lost keys
one more time.

❧

26

that getting the kids ready
for church is not just the
woman's responsibility.

❧

27

how to forgive others.

❧

28

that it is okay
to admit he was wrong . . .
at least once.

❦

29

that arrogance is ugly.

❦

30

how to tell ten great Bible
stories to his children.

31

when it is best to keep his
mouth shut.

32

that there are women
who are much smarter
than he is.

33

that letting the sun go
down on his anger often
makes things worse.

how to use more kitchen appliances than just the refrigerator and the microwave.

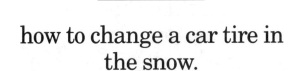

how to change a car tire in the snow.

36

when he is spending too much time at the office and not enough time at home.

37

to empty the trash before it overflows.

that his children watch his
walk with the Lord.

that giving his loved one a
pet as a gift is a decision he
will pay for later.

40

at least one way to
tie a necktie.

41

how to fold a map
and drive the car at the
same time.

how to wash the dishes.

how to throw a
curveball.

44

nightly prayers with his children will never be a waste of time.

45

how to build a kite from scratch.

46

_____

blaming the boss does
nothing for his job security.

47

_____

how to ensure his income
is greater than his
expenditures.

love notes left around the
house make for a good
homecoming later in
the evening.

how to change the oil in
the car.

50

that all work and no play
will make him very boring.

51

how to stomach
amusement-park rides.

52

the birthdate of his wife
or girlfriend.

❧

53

the price of a dozen roses.

❧

54

people at his
high school reunion
will be too excited about
seeing him to bother
noticing he has become
fat and bald.

55

how to hang up his
own clothes.

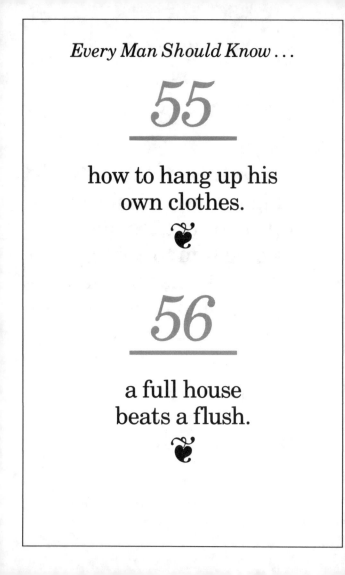

56

a full house
beats a flush.

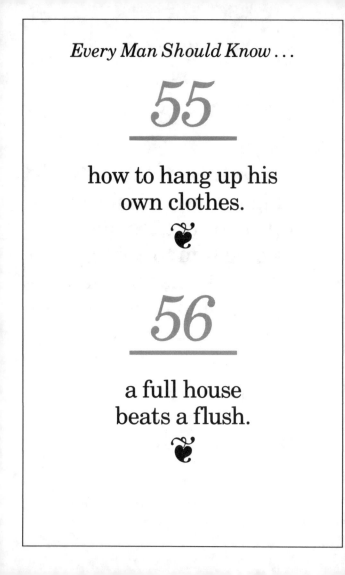

Every Man Should Know . . .

married men can have
single male buddies, and
single men can have
married male friends.

58

which grocery stores take
double coupons.

❦

59

that if he has a wife, he
should not have a
girlfriend.

❦

60

it can be cheaper to
call a plumber than to
repair it himself.

61

how to convert
measurements to the
metric system.

62

how to properly carve
a turkey.

63

at least a dozen ways to
have fun with his children.

---

a woman likes a man in
a bathrobe.

---

that surprise gifts provide
long-term memories.

66

how to laugh in the midst
of a crisis.

67

that the best boss is the
one who cares.

that sometimes he may
have to face his fears in
order to stand up for
what is right.

69

how to set up a tent in a
strong wind.

70

that he does not need to
use foul language.

71

there is never a "perfect"
time to take a vacation.

72

whom to call when he
gets depressed.

73

sometimes his wallet
needs to be controlled
by his heart rather than
his head.

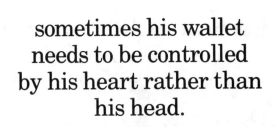

Every Man Should Know . . .

74

his neighbor's wife has
stretch marks, too.

❧

75

how to tie a Christmas tree
to the roof of a car.

❧

76

the birthdates of his
children.

77

when it is time to trim the
hair coming out of his ears
(or nose).

78

how to recognize the difference between weeds and a flower that has not yet bloomed.

79

Valentine's Day is always an important holiday.

80

how to lose the
"love handles" before
summer arrives.

❧

81

how to make a
rope swing.

❧

82

how to use different
voices while reading
children's stories.

83

his wife's or girlfriend's
favorite flavor of ice cream.

that wasting time over
insignificant details is not
worth his time.

beauty is only skin-deep.

86

how to listen more and
talk less.

❧

87

women think very
differently than men.

❧

88

that it is okay to cry.

89

that spiritual leadership
at home is more important
than climbing the ladder
at work.

90

anger expressed slowly can
defuse a defensive spirit.

❦

91

children need to see their
father show affection
toward their mother.

❦

92

how to build
a good relationship with
his in-laws.

93

dirty socks left on the floor
cannot walk to the hamper
on their own.

the penalty for an
out-of-bounds golf ball is
two strokes.

his good looks are a gift
from God.

96

how to boil an egg.

❦

97

the best places to go for
a picnic.

❦

Every Man Should Know . . .

98

how to keep his
room clean.

❧

99

it is important to lower the
toilet seat if women share
the home.

❧

100

it is okay if he doesn't
understand football
terminology.

101

saying "I love you" is not
enough if he doesn't spend
time with her too.

102

a handy notepad can save a
fading memory.

103

bigotry and prejudice make
the world a little darker.

how to talk the neighbor
kid into mowing the lawn
so he won't miss the
seventh game of the
World Series.

105

how to change the washers
on the sink or shower
fixtures.

106

several alternate routes to
and from work.

107

negative talk
about his wife, in front
of the children, can
hurt them deeply.

108

how to build and start
a campfire.

109

that his parents would like
him to call once in a while.

110

how to put the
Christmas tree in the
stand so it doesn't lean
and it can get water.

111

giving a Bible to a family
member may be the gift of
a lifetime.

112

the best place to watch
planes take off and land.

113

how to give a good tip to a great waiter or waitress.

114

how to iron a shirt in less than five minutes.

115

when he is in the
doghouse—and how
to get out.

116

which is her favorite
station on the radio.

to warn his wife when "the boys" are coming over to watch football.

118

how to carve a jack-o'-lantern.

119

the love verses in
1 Corinthians 13
by heart . . . and try to
live by them.

120

the patterns of family
dysfunction can be broken.

121

that greed is a destructive weed that can choke out growth in a relationship.

122

he can save money on shampoo by bringing it home from hotel rooms.

his children will learn
more from what he does
than from what he says.

the words to the national
anthem.

125

that gifts are usually more
important to females
than to males.

126

church offering plates
accept folding money as
well as change.

to surprise his "special
someone" with a daytime
phone interruption.

when to say he is sorry.

129

how to entertain small
children with magic tricks
and juggling acts.

❧

130

that magazine photos of
beautiful women are
airbrushed.

❧

how to be liberal with
his praise.

how to balance his time
among family, friends,
work, church, and
recreation.

133

how honorable it is to be
called a man of integrity
among your peers and
co-workers.

134

where his car registration
is located.

135

how to help his children
financially without
spoiling them.

136

he should not look
in a woman's purse
without asking.

the rubber band
around the newspaper
should be shot at
something every day.

how to wrap a present.

139

silence is not golden when
he is angry.

140

the good silverware
usually does not go in the
same drawer as the
everyday utensils.

141

the number of pints in
a gallon.

142

that women love to
cuddle . . . without it
leading to sex.

143

she probably
doesn't appreciate him
using the same plunger
for the kitchen sink
that he just used
in the toilet.

that pride
isn't a character trait he
wants to pass on to his
children, but rather,
humility.

to occasionally spend time
in solitude.

not to eat unshelled
peanuts in the living room.

147

to pay others fairly.

148

there are kinder ways to
break off a romance than
to simply quit calling her.

149

it is proper for him to get on and off an elevator before the ladies so that he is the one who trips in case the floor is not flush with the elevator.

the one who dies with the
most toys does not win.

women do not like sports to
replace their presence.

how to show
a glimpse of God's grace
to others in his life.

what day the
trashman comes.

how to sit through
a mushy movie with her,
since she was willing to
sit through all the
Rambo movies with him.

155

words *can* hurt more than
sticks and stones.

156

what his health
insurance covers.

157

clocks are set ahead in the spring and turned back in the fall.

❦

158

how to be kind to animals.

❦

159

a season beginning at 0-1
can still finish 11-1.

160

his wife's or girlfriend's
favorite time of the year.

161

how to give a eulogy for a
close friend.

162

sissy is not the root word
for *sensitivity*.

how to forgive himself for his past.

that it is easier for a baby to say Dada than to say Mama.

165

she may be in the mood
when he isn't . . . but it's
not likely.

166

how to remain calm when
cut off by bad drivers.

Bo Derek will not always
be a 10.

the importance of dating
his spouse even after
marriage.

Every Man Should Know . . .

169

the stages of pregnancy.

170

how to tolerate his
teenagers when they act
like he did at that age.

171

the importance of keeping
an appointment book
up-to-date.

172

how to tell his "significant
other" the truth when she
asks, "How was your day?"

173

the greatest leaps of growth often come after times of great pain.

174

at least ten things he can do regularly to save the environment.

175

how to shave
without leaving patches
of whiskers on his
face and neck.

176

how to row a boat.

177

spending time with loved
ones is more important
than spending time with
golf clubs.

178

only Jesus can walk
on water.

179

her problems will not go
away just because she now
has an engagement ring.

180

not everyone wants to hear
about his kids all the time.

181

some women still
appreciate having doors
opened for them.

❧

182

how to throw a frisbee.

❧

his vote is important.

just because everyone
else is doing it
doesn't necessarily
make it right.

when her "time of the
month" will arrive.

that women
think men have a
"time of the month" too.

187

the birthdates of his
siblings.

188

how to make a
meaningful toast.

189

he doesn't have to act just
like his dad.

190

he probably watches too
much television.

191

that consistent devotions
with his family are wise
investments.

192

to respect other people's
property more than he
does his own.

Every Man Should Know . . .

193

how to accept women
who see their role
in life differently
than he sees it.

Every Man Should Know . . .

how to start planning
for retirement.

when he needs
professional help.

196

how to put chains on the
car in a snowstorm.

197

an escape plan when he
realizes his zipper is open
while in public.

198

it is an inevitable fact that
he will spill lunch on his
new necktie the first day
he wears it.

199

the women in his life
probably know more than
he thinks they do.

200

he can benefit from
being accountable to
another man.

how to use logic in
making decisions.

how to double-tie a
child's shoes.

203

when it is time to get
a haircut.

204

a white lie is still a lie—
no matter how little.

impotence has a
solution.

the proper thing to wear
at a social function.

as many nursery rhymes
as possible.

his mother-in-law's
birthday.

209

he can glean more wisdom
from reading "Peanuts"
and "Dear Abby" than
from memorizing the
statistics in the
sports section.

210

which books are in the Old Testament and which ones are in the New Testament.

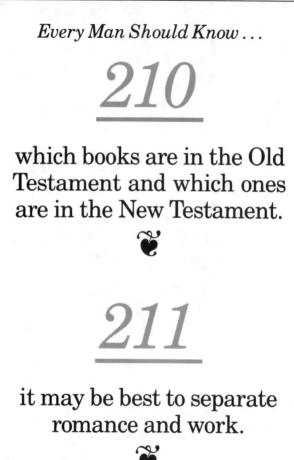

211

it may be best to separate romance and work.

he can be a whole person
whether he is single
or married.

how to display the fruit
of the Spirit.

214

how to find at least two
constellations among
the stars.

215

today may be the last time
he sees someone he loves.

216

the importance
of regularly spending
time alone with each
family member.

217

he should never ask a
woman her age or weight.

when he is in denial of his addictions.

how to keep score in bowling.

where the water and gas
mains are located.

Playboy has a lot more
than great articles . . . and
women know it.

the best way to
lose friends and employees
is to control them.

how to spit-shine
his shoes.

how to build a
model airplane.

the ages of his
children.

how to dye Easter eggs.

227

just the right thing to say
when she is really mad.

228

a trip to the local
greasy-spoon
sports bar is not
her idea of a
romantic dinner.

the kids who
bullied him as a child
are now much lesser men
than he.

230

no one is perfect—
including himself.

231

commitments are made
to be kept.

232

how to read
military rank.

❧

233

the duties of being a
best man.

❧

his shoe, pants, shirt, and
suit sizes.

empathy is not an emotion
reserved only for the
female species.

236

it is best to read the
instructions before
he begins.

237

women enjoy a
new outfit for the big event
or special occasion.

238

how to build intriguing
sand castles.

239

the proper place to trim his
toenails and where to put
the remains.

240

"Because" does not satisfy
the child who asks,
"Why?"

241

how to be a servant to
other people.

Every Man Should Know...

how to ask for directions
when lost.

how to be creative on
a date.

244

how to cope when he
doesn't get things his way.

245

he should not continue to
eat when he is full.

246

when he compares
himself to others, there
will always be someone
who is better-looking,
wealthier, and seemingly
happier.

the words to his loved one's
favorite song.

what clothes to wash
together when doing
the laundry.

249

at least five stories that
can make himself and
other people laugh.

250

to keep a current picture of
his family in his wallet.

251

the best method for getting
a stain out of the carpet.

252

the only men who should
pat other men on the fanny
are professional athletes.

how to keep something
confidential when it has
been shared as such.

she still wants to
hold hands—even after
the honeymoon.

255

how to hang
wallpaper.

256

how to bait a
fishhook.

257

gray hair makes him look
distinguished—not old.

258

how to accept the
consequences of
being wrong.

259

a friend going through
a divorce needs your
friendship more than ever.

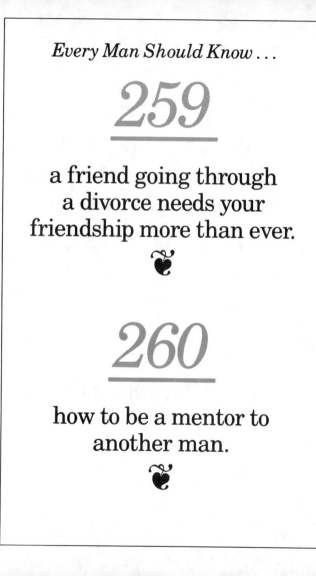

260

how to be a mentor to
another man.

Every Man Should Know . . .

261

how to give CPR.

262

his wife still loves him
when the first child comes,
even though it seems the
child is getting all
her attention.

263

he should not go to work
for a friend unless he is
willing to risk losing the
friendship.

264

she really means no when
she says no.

how to show an interest in
his loved one's hobbies.

how to help a stranger
in need.

267

he should spend more time
with people than he does
with his computer.

268

at least ten different ways
of saying "I love you."

when to get new tires
for the car.

real men do eat quiche.

271

whether to use masking,
scotch, or electrical tape in
any given situation.

❦

272

how to record a program
on the VCR.

❦

273

which of his friends would
come to his side if he
became seriously ill.

274

how to listen to the snap,
crackle, and pop with
his children.

275

a good place to go
and neck.

276

how to make a bachelor
pad not look like a
bachelor pad.

277

the birthdates of his
parents.

278

other people do not exist
for the purpose of meeting
his needs or filling
his wallet.

279

ways to kill the spider on
the wall without leaving
a mark.

280

the importance of having
a savings account for
emergencies.

Tom Selleck is getting
wrinkles, too.

sexual promiscuity is not
on the resumé for a
healthy man.

283

his dentist really will try
to be gentle.

284

he usually cannot go
another 75 miles after the
fuel light comes on.

285

a good way for a single
man to meet women is to
go for a walk with his cute
baby niece, nephew,
or puppy.

286

the color of his wife's eyes.

five feet, ten inches does
not equal six feet.

the advice he hears from
other people is not
always right.

289

women love
surprise gifts.

290

if he is too busy to help
his kids when they ask
for it, they may end up
too busy for him.

291

the best traditions to pass on are those that make him feel warm and fuzzy.

❦

292

how to interpret his children's drawings.

❦

293

Hawaiian shirts do not go
with plaid pants.

294

how to comfort his wife
when she is sick.

295

he should not put
the newspaper on a
white couch.

296

drinking the "right" beer is
not going to get him the
right woman.

he needs both a Phillips
and a standard, flat
screwdriver in the house.

when to throw out his
favorite old T-shirt.

299

the names of the
seven dwarves.

300

how to make those around
him feel appreciated.

301

his best friend from high
school would be thrilled to
get a phone call from him.

302

he needs to be there
when his teenager's heart
is broken.

303

the only men who should
scratch themselves in
public are baseball players.

❦

304

how to spend regular time
in prayer alone and with
other people.

❦

305

if he has a 10 o'clock
appointment with the
doctor, he should not expect
to be seen until 11 o'clock.

306

how to paint a room.

that whatever he has not
touched for a year can
probably be considered
junk and thrown out.

the pros and cons of buying
term life insurance.

309

a job loss can turn into the greatest lesson that ever happened to him.

310

how to get rid of little habits that annoy those nearest to him.

311

several ways to spend a
rainy day.

❧

312

how to build at least one
Lego masterpiece.

❧

Every Man Should Know . . .

313

which way is north, south,
east, and west.

314

silk plants do not need to
be watered.

Every Man Should Know . . .

315

that drinking and driving
is downright stupid.

❧

316

the importance of
volunteering time to help
the poor.

❧

317

how much kids like going
to the circus.

318

how to take a decent
photograph.

319

Christmas is not only
for children.

320

it is okay
to be late . . .
when he calls ahead.

to stop at the antique store
in an out-of-town
neighborhood.

a little cologne goes
a long way.

323

some people really do
watch professional bowling
on television.

❧

324

if the suit does not fit, do
not wear it.

❧

325

the love of one woman is
far more attractive than
the love of many.

326

God hears songs of praise
louder than lousy singing.

327

when life ends he will never regret the times he left work early to be with his family.

❦

328

how to cook for more than one person.

❦

329

a soda with two straws can mean more to her than champagne.

330

sensitivity, ambition, and confidence are attractive.

331

---

black socks look stupid
with short pants.

332

---

white socks look stupid
with black pants.

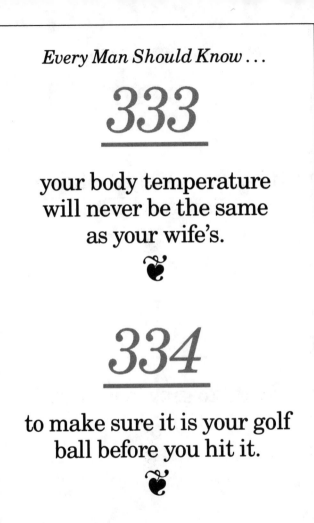

333

your body temperature
will never be the same
as your wife's.

334

to make sure it is your golf
ball before you hit it.

Every Man Should Know . . .

335

that even Magic Johnson
can get AIDS.

336

how to grow a garden.

337

how to be a
great mother, too.

338

how to throw a
surprise party.

339

tattoos are permanent.

340

saying "You look fine"
to her rarely registers on
the compliment scale.

341

how to keep the Sabbath holy and not filled with appointments.

342

how to graciously give up his umbrella, sports coat, and last bite of dessert.

Every Man Should Know . . .

dumb-blonde jokes are not
funny to blondes.

how to make homemade
ice cream.

the greater value in
becoming a human being
instead of a human doing.

a wet washcloth
in the dryer cures
the common wrinkle.

347

back rubs are one cure
for anger.

348

how to travel without
packing too much.

349

a scenic drive can become
a fun adventure.

350

that he should never hit
another human being.

Every Man Should Know . . .

351

admitting a weakness is
not being weak.

❧

352

the phrase "lived in" does
not translate to "sloppy."

❧

353

he can blame it
on the dog for only a
limited amount of time.

354

a hat and a little deodorant
can replace a shower when
in a hurry.

body language can shout
to some.

the date of his boss'
birthday.

357

the best place to view the
fall colors.

358

to pray specifically.

359

responsibility
needs to be taught
and not assumed.

360

the best wedding gifts
are the ones on the
gift registry.

361

how to help with
homework without
actually doing it.

362

how to identify the motive
behind his bragging.

363

how to install a
swing set.

364

a game to play
with his children
during an important
phone call.

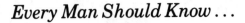

Every Man Should Know . . .

365

how to tell his dad
he loves him.

About the Author

Doug Fields, founder and director of *Making Young Lives Count*, is a national public speaker, college professor, and author of over 12 books including *Creative Romance* and *Too Old, Too Soon*. He serves as director of youth ministry at Saddleback Valley Community Church in Mission Viejo, California.

For further information regarding *Making Young Lives Count* or a brochure of more resources, please call or write Doug Fields at:

Making Young Lives Count
4330 Barranca Parkway
Suite 101-346
Irvine, CA 92714
(714) 651-1942

Where to look in the Bible....

When you need rest and peace,
  read Matthew 11:25-30.
When you worry, read Matthew 6:19-34
When you are lonely or fearful, read Psalm 23.
When you need peace of mind,
  read John 14:47; Phillippians 4:6-8.
When men fail you, read Psalm 27.
When you grow bitter or critical,
  read 1 Corinthians 13.
When you have sinned, read Psalm 51; 1 John 1.
When you are discourage, read Psalm 34.
When God seems far away, read Psalm 139.
When the world seems bigger than God,
  read Psalm 90.
When in sickness, read Psalm 41.
When you feel sorrowful,
  read John 14; Psalm 46.
When in danger, read Psalm 91.
When you want courage, read Joshua 1:1-9.
When you need assurance, read Romans 8.
When you forget your blessings,
  read Psalm 103.
When looking for joy, read Colossians 3.
When you leave home to travel, read Psalm 121.
When you think of investments,
  read Mark 10:17-31.
When you need guidelines for living,
  read Matthew 5-7; Romans 12.
When you need rules of conduct,
  read Exodus 20:1-17.
When you need to know God's will for your life,
  read Proverbs 3:1-6.